Name:_____ Date._____

a a a a a

a a a a a

a a a a a

a a a a a

a a a a a

a a a a a

A is for alligator.

A is for alligator.

A is for alligator.

A is for alligator.

A is for alligator.

A is for alligator.

Name:_____ Date:_____

B is for basketball

B is for basketball

B is for basketball

B is for basketball

B is for basketball

B is for basketball

Name:_____ Date:_____

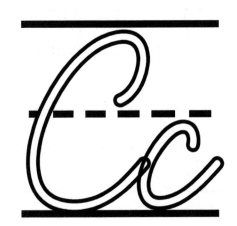

C ccccc

c ccccc

C ccccc

c ccccc

C is for caterpillars

C is for caterpillars

C is for caterpillars

C is for caterpillars

C is for caterpillars

C is for caterpillars

Name:_____ Date:_____

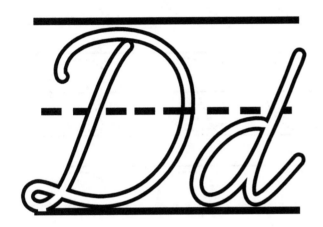

D is for doughnuts.

D is for doughnuts.

D is for doughnuts.

D is for doughnuts.

D is for doughnuts.

D is for doughnuts.

Name:_____ Date:_____

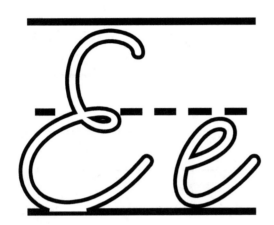

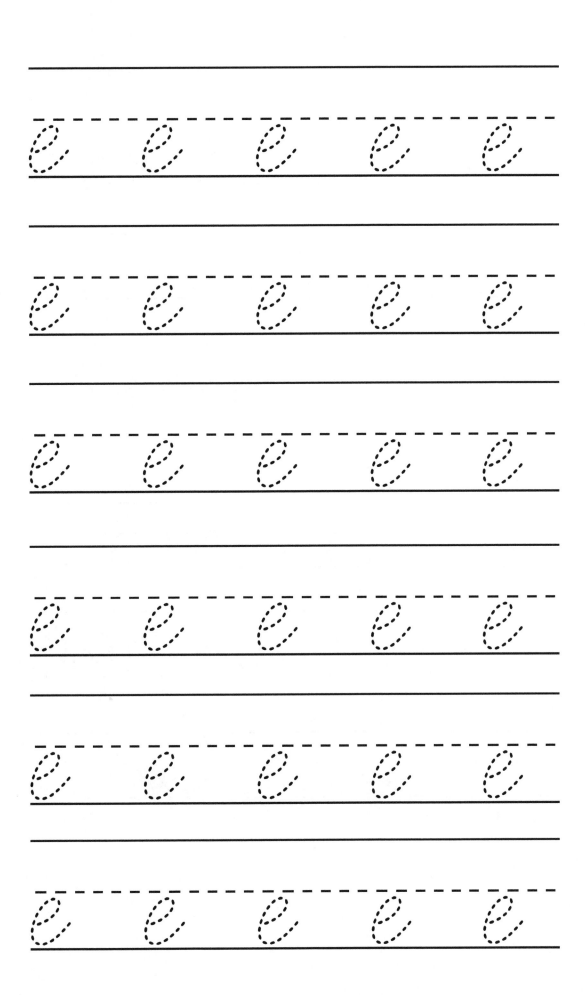

E is for elephants.

E is for elephants.

E is for elephants.

E is for elephants.

E is for elephants.

E is for elephants.

Name:_____ Date:_____

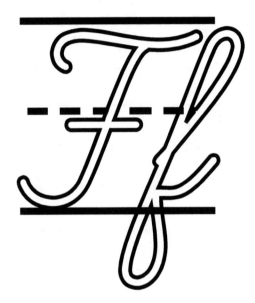

F is for funny.

F is for funny.

F is for funny.

F is for funny.

F is for funny.

F is for funny.

Name:_____ Date:_____

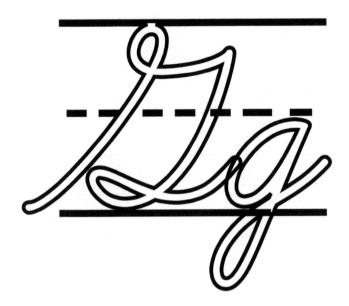

G is for girls.

G is for girls.

G is for girls.

G is for girls.

G is for girls.

G is for girls.

Name:_____ Date:_____

It is for hotdogs.
It is for hotdogs.
It is for hotdogs.

It is for hotdogs.
It is for hotdogs.
It is for hotdogs.

Name:_____ Date:_____

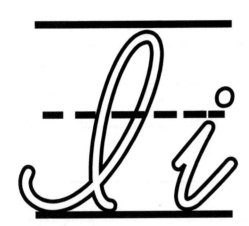

l l l l l l

i i i i i i i i i

l l l l l l

i i i i i i i i i

I is for ice-cream.

I is for ice-cream.

I is for ice-cream.

I is for ice-cream.

I is for ice-cream.

I is for ice-cream.

Name:_____ Date:_____

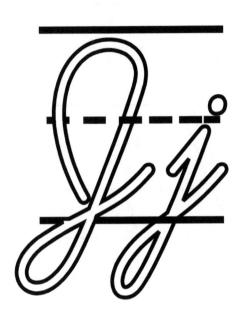

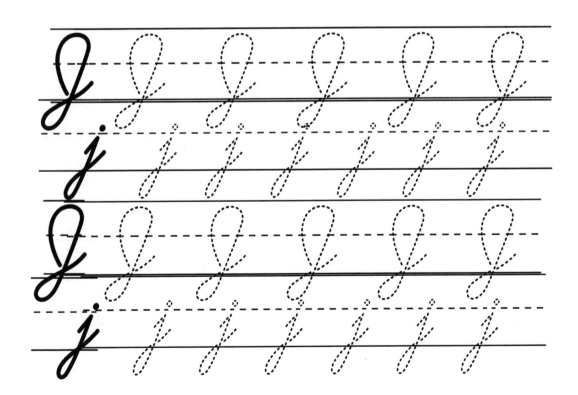

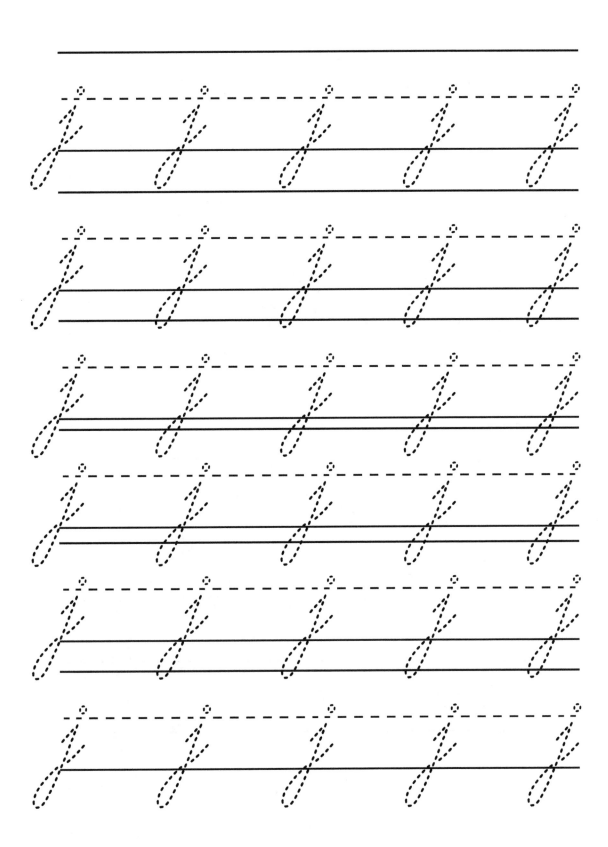

J is for jumping.

J is for jumping.

J is for jumping.

J is for jumping.

J is for jumping.

J is for jumping.

Name:_____ Date:_____

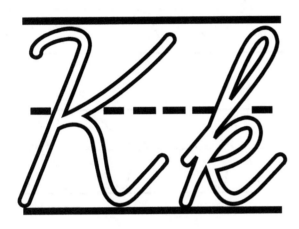

(Deuteronomy 5:12)

Keep the Sabbath day holy, exactly as the Lord your God commanded thee.

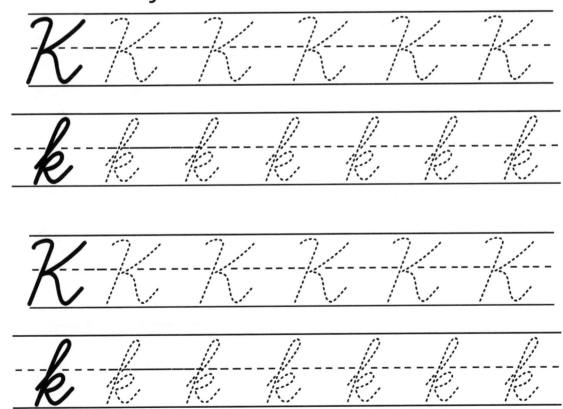

K is for kickball.

K is for kickball.

K is for kickball.

K is for kickball.

K is for kickball.

K is for kickball.

Name:_____ Date:_____

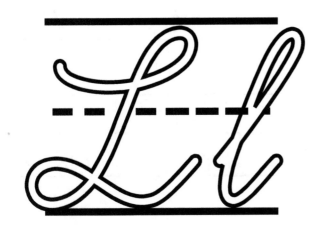

L is for lollipop.

L is for lollipop.

L is for lollipop.

L is for lollipop.

L is for lollipop.

L is for lollipop.

Name:_____ Date:_____

m m m m m

m m m m m

m m m m m

m m m m m

m m m m m

m m m m m

m m m m m

m m m m m

m m m m m

m m m m m

m m m m m

m m m m m

M is for mother.

M is for mother.

M is for mother.

M is for mother.

M is for mother.

M is for mother.

Name:_____ Date:_____

n n n n n

n n n n n

n n n n n

n n n n n

n n n n n

n n n n n

N is for nickel.

N is for nickel.

N is for nickel.

N is for nickel.

N is for nickel.

N is for nickel.

Name:_____ Date:_____

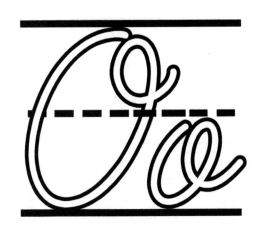

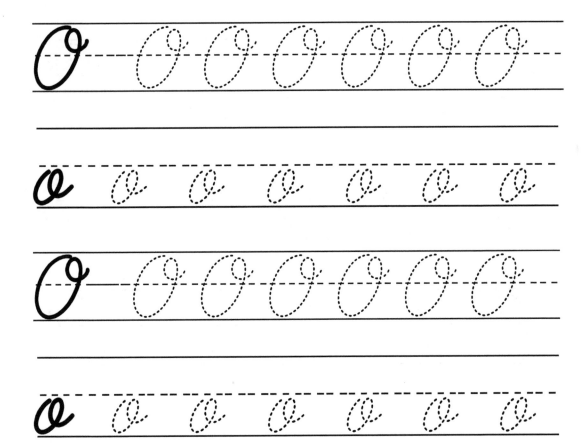

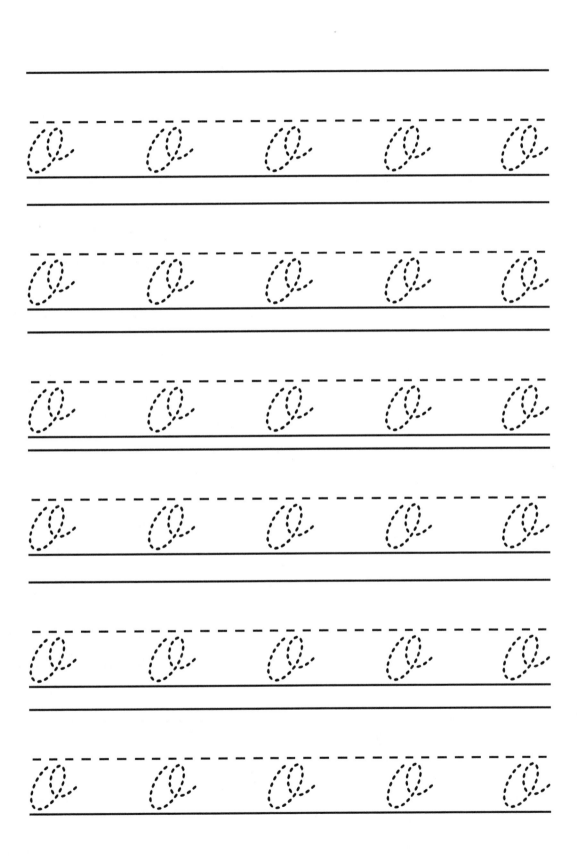

O is for octopus.

O is for octopus.

O is for octopus.

O is for octopus.

O is for octopus.

O is for octopus.

Name:_____ Date:_____

p p p p p

p p p p p

p p p p p

p p p p p

p p p p p

p p p p p

p p p p p

p p p p p

p p p p p

p p p p p

p p p p p

p p p p p

P is for pepperonis.

P is for pepperonis.

P is for pepperonis.

P is for pepperonis.

P is for pepperonis.

P is for pepperonis.

Name:_____ Date:_____

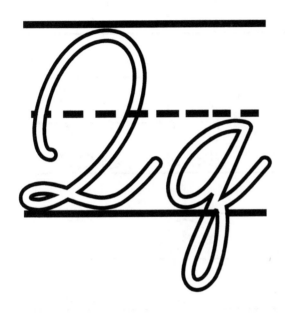

Q is for queen.

Q is for queen.

Q is for queen.

Q is for queen.

Q is for queen.

Q is for queen.

Name:_____ Date:_____

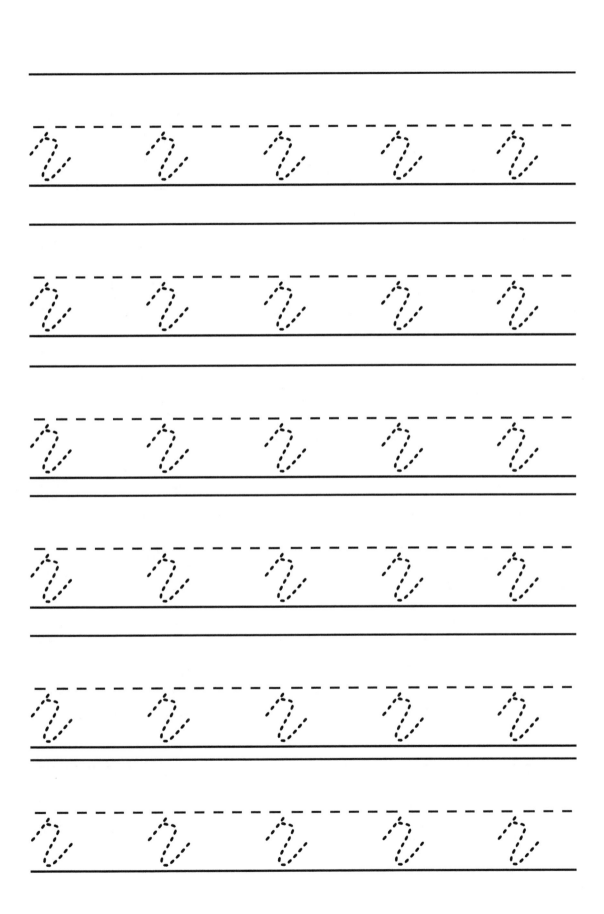

R is for rainbow.

R is for rainbow.

R is for rainbow.

R is for rainbow.

R is for rainbow.

R is for rainbow.

Name:_____ Date:_____

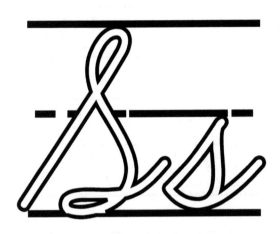

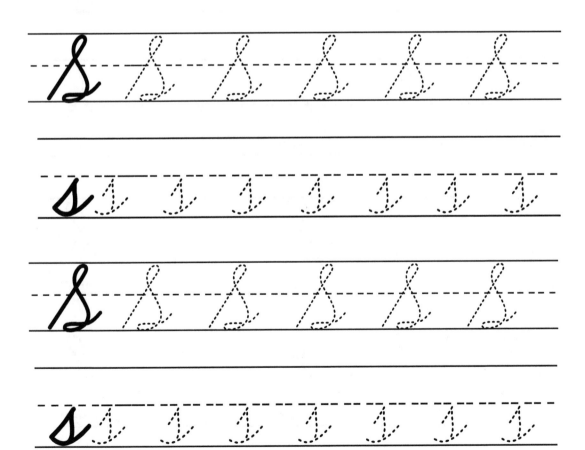

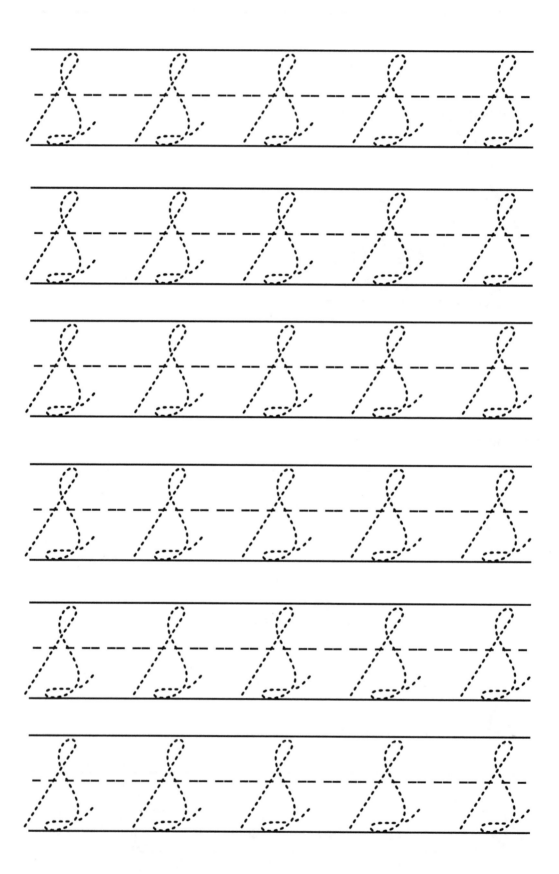

S is for sunshine.

S is for sunshine.

S is for sunshine.

S is for sunshine.

S is for sunshine.

S is for sunshine.

Name:_____ Date:_____

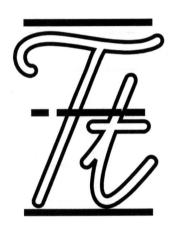

T is for terrific!

T is for terrific!

T is for terrific!

T is for terrific!

T is for terrific!

T is for terrific!

Name:_____ Date:_____

U is for umbrella

U is for umbrella

U is for umbrella

U is for umbrella

U is for umbrella

U is for umbrella

Name:_____ Date:_____

u u u u u

u u u u u

u u u u u

u u u u u

u u u u u

u u u u u

V is for violin.

V is for violin.

V is for violin.

V is for violin.

V is for violin.

V is for violin.

Name:_____ Date:_____

W is for wheel.

W is for wheel.

W is for wheel.

W is for wheel.

W is for wheel.

W is for wheel.

Name:_____ Date:_____

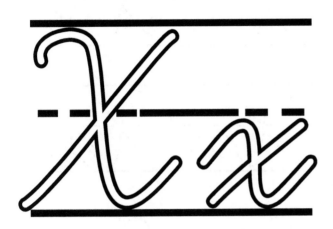

Xx Xx Xx Xx

Xx Xx Xx Xx

Xx Xx Xx Xx

Xx Xx Xx Xx

Xx Xx Xx Xx

Xx Xx Xx Xx

X is for X-Ray.
X is for X-Ray.
X is for X-Ray.
X is for X-Ray.
X is for X-Ray.
X is for X-Ray.

Name:_____ Date:_____

Yy Yy Yy Yy Yy

Yy Yy Yy Yy Yy

Yy Yy Yy Yy Yy

Yy Yy Yy Yy Yy

Yy Yy Yy Yy Yy

Yy Yy Yy Yy Yy

Name:_____ Date:_____

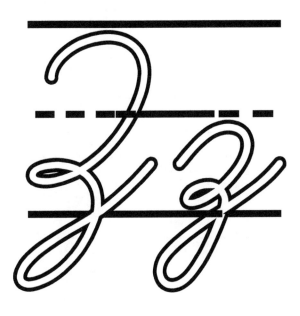

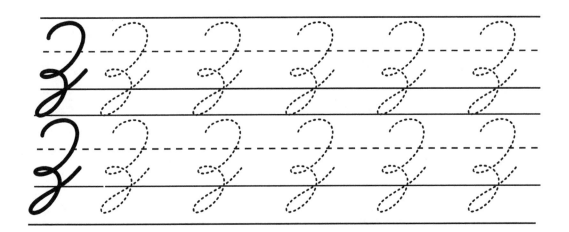

Name: Date:

Tracing Letters

Practice tracing the sight words below.

are   above   another   at

about   above   easy   enough

first   found   float   listen

make   made   more   many

second   since   sometimes

said   saw   they   thing

usually   use   write   when

Name: **Date:**

Tracing Numbers

1	2	3	4
5	6	7	8
9	10	11	12
13	14	15	16
17	18	19	20
21	22	23	24

Name: Date:

Tracing Numbers

Practice cursive writing by tracing the numbers below.

25 26 27 28

29 30 31 32

33 34 35 36

37 38 39 40

41 42 43 44

45 46 47 48

49 50

Name: Date:

Tracing Numbers

Practice cursive writing by tracing the numbers below.

51	52	53	54
55	56	57	58
59	60	61	62
63	64	65	66
67	68	69	70
71	72	73	74
75	76		

Name: Date:

Tracing Numbers

Practice cursive writing by tracing the numbers below.

77	78	79	80
81	82	83	84
84	85	86	87
88	89	90	91
92	93	94	95
96	97	98	99
100			

Name: Date:

Tracing Letters

Practice writing the alphabet by tracing the letters below.

Aa	Bb	Cc	Dd
Ee	Ff	Gg	Hh
Ii	Jj	Kk	Ll
Mm	Nn	Oo	Pp
Qq	Rr	Ss	Tt
Uu	Vv	Ww	Xx
Yy	Zz		

Name: Date:

Tracing Letters

Practice writing the alphabet by tracing the letters below.

Aa Bb Cc Dd

Ee Ff Gg Hh

Ii Jj Kk Ll

Mm Nn Oo Pp

Qq Rr Ss Tt

Uu Vv Ww Xx

Yy Zz

Name: Date:

Tracing Letters

Practice writing the alphabet by tracing the letters below.

Aa Bb Cc Dd

Ee Ff Gg Hh

Ii Jj Kk Ll

Mm Nn Oo Pp

Qq Rr Ss Tt

Uu Vv Ww Xx

Yy Zz

Name: Date:

Tracing Letters

Practice writing the alphabet by tracing the letters below.

Aa Bb Cc Dd

Ee Ff Gg Hh

Ii Jj Kk Ll

Mm Nn Oo Pp

Qq Rr Ss Tt

Uu Vv Ww Xx

Yy Zz

Name: Date:

Tracing Letters

Practice writing the alphabet by tracing the letters below.

Aa	Bb	Cc	Dd
Ee	Ff	Gg	Hh
Ii	Jj	Kk	Ll
Mm	Nn	Oo	Pp
Qq	Rr	Ss	Tt
Uu	Vv	Ww	Xx
Yy	Zz		

Name: Date:

Tracing Letters

Practice writing the alphabet by tracing the letters below.

Aa   Bb   Cc   Dd

Ee   Ff   Gg   Hh

Ii   Jj   Kk   Ll

Mm   Nn   Oo   Pp

Qq   Rr   Ss   Tt

Uu   Vv   Ww   Xx

Yy   Zz

Name: Date:

Tracing Letters

Practice writing the alphabet by tracing the letters below.

Aa Bb Cc Dd

Ee Ff Gg Hh

Ii Jj Kk Ll

Mm Nn Oo Pp

Qq Rr Ss Tt

Uu Vv Ww Xx

Yy Zz

Name: Date:

Tracing Letters

Practice writing the alphabet by tracing the letters below.

Aa Bb Cc Dd

Ee Ff Gg Hh

Ii Jj Kk Ll

Mm Nn Oo Pp

Qq Rr Ss Tt

Uu Vv Ww Xx

Yy Zz

Name: Date:

Tracing Letters

Practice writing the alphabet by tracing the letters below.

Aa Bb Cc Dd

Ee Ff Gg Hh

Ii Jj Kk Ll

Mm Nn Oo Pp

Qq Rr Ss Tt

Uu Vv Ww Xx

Yy Zz

Name: Date:

Tracing Letters

Practice writing the alphabet by tracing the letters below.

Aa Bb Cc Dd

Ee Ff Gg Hh

Ii Jj Kk Ll

Mm Nn Oo Pp

Qq Rr Ss Tt

Uu Vv Ww Xx

Yy Zz